JOSIAH **KE**

# DEBTLESS

## HELPING STUDENTS TAKE ON LESS DEBT

FOREWORD BY **JERRID SEBESTA**

# DEBTLESS
Helping Students Take on Less Debt
By: Josiah Kennealy

## PRAISE FOR DEBTLESS

"Financial literacy with a heart and a conscience! Josiah Kennealy's text *Debtless* is a gift and a guide for our young scholars. To emerge from the college academic journey with the ability to focus on professional passions of the heart without excessive debt will set you free. *Debtless* is a warm and practical springboard to the reader's future!"
—Dr. Randall Peterson, Principal, Eastview High School

"*Debtless* is a short book that will help parents and students as they assess how to have a college education without being saddled by debt. Josiah Kennealy illustrates from his own experience how to go through college debt free. Each chapter has practical questions that parents and students can work through as they financially plan for a college or university education."
—Dr. George O. Wood, General Superintendent, The General Council of the Assemblies of God

"This outstanding book by Josiah Kennealy is about fiscal destiny. Reckless student indebtedness is killing a generation before it even has a chance to start. Finally, we have in Josiah Kennealy, a 'prophet to his peers' who gives all of us, both young and old, a new vision and story for how to pay for college. His newest book, *Debtless*, delivers big time."
—Dr. Scott Hagan, President, North Central University

"Dreams are fueled by reality. Reality is that money can be a weight, as in value, or a weight, as in burden. Josiah helps you do the heavy lifting so your dreams have weight and value as you navigate what can be a burden."
—Eric Samuel Timm, Author of *Static Jedi*, Artist with *Painting Hope*, Orator, Visionary

"Scholastic debt is one of the greatest challenges facing this generation of students. *Debtless* will equip students of all ages and backgrounds to make wise decisions that will profoundly impact their future."
—Mark Dean, District Youth Director, Minnesota District Council of the Assemblies of God

"It can be done! You can graduate debt free and the principles Josiah shares can be applied to everyday life for anyone. Be curious, educate yourself, find a mentor, have courage, and begin the journey to a debtless future."
—Roger Lane, Stewardship Coach, True North Strategies Group

"Josiah knows how to dream big dreams. He has a 'giant' to kill that is much bigger than he is. In this book, he tackles the giant of debt, and wins. You will love this book!"
—Clarence W. St. John, Superintendent, Minnesota District Council of the Assemblies of God

"I highly respect the character and judgment Josiah has displayed throughout his ministry. He's consistently invested in the next generation, believing in their potential and purpose. This book is a critical tool for the next generation to accomplish their purpose. Without it, the weight of debt will kill their dreams. I recommend this book to be read by anyone ready to run free."
—Nate Ruch, Lead Pastor, Emmanuel Christian Center

"College has enough twist and turns without having to tackle its price tag. As unnavigable as it may seem, *Debtless* gives such practical, ready-to-use wisdom leaving you to set your sights on a debt free journey."
—Ryan Koster, College Pastor, University of Minnesota Chi Alpha

"I have personally known Josiah for almost eight years. This is someone who has gotten through college and grad school without debt—he's not some trust fund baby. This is real world stuff. In this book, you're going to hear and read the real-life experience of someone who's been there. This is a must-read for anyone considering higher education!"
—Neal J. Rich, Lead Pastor, Cedar Valley Church

"What I love about Josiah's no-nonsense approach to tackling debt is that his perspectives are proactive and not reactive. The outcomes of his research shine a light on the epidemic of academic debt, but what shines brighter are the solutions he brings so that an individual can avoid debt altogether. Every student should have this in their hands!"
—Terry Parkman, NextGen Pastor, River Valley Church

"Josiah Kennealy loves Jesus and loves people and *Debtless* is an extension of these truths. Whether you're seeking freedom in your finances or simply wanting to start on the right foot, this book is an incredible resource from a leader who cares."
—Nick Hall, Founder of PULSE and Together 2016, Author of Reset: Jesus Changes Everything

"If 'education is the key to success', then Debtless is the locksmith that can unlock the potential of a low debt or completely debtless college experience. Josiah Kennealy speaks to the subject matter of Debtless with great authority as he has personally lived out the ten tips to graduate with THREE degrees (AA, BA, MA) completely debt-free. Every prospective college student would benefit greatly from reading Debtless and implementing the ten simple tips for minimizing debt. College should be about amassing education and experiences, not debt!"

—Brent Silkey, College Pastor | Founder of 30 for Freedom

## DEDICATION

To my parents. You have been in my corner, praying for me, and supporting me since the day I was born.

To my soon-to-be wife, Micah. You are my forever bride, best friend, prayer warrior, and encourager.

To this generation. May you find financial freedom so you can pursue every passion, dream, and endeavor you have in your heart.

# CONTENTS

**FOREWARD**
By Jerrid Sebesta
#LivinTheDream


In 2014, after I abruptly left my TV career of 12 years, I was asked two questions over and over again: "Why?" followed quickly by "How?"

The "why" was simple. My wife and I felt called to a simpler life with more family time and less media time—more purpose and less status.

You see, when I left my job, I voluntarily walked into unemployment. I had no other job or form of income lined-up. My wife was a full time stay-at-home mother. Oh, and did I mention we were pregnant with our third child? Not surprisingly, many people in the general public assumed I was crazy, especially considering my nonchalant attitude about where or when my next paycheck would be coming.

So, "how" then?

I was *Debtless*.

This book really isn't about money. It's about life. It's about freedom. Being *Debtless* is about power—the power to chase the life you're called to live.

Unfortunately, most Americans are not free. As many as 70% of Americans live paycheck-to-paycheck. The easiest way I know for someone to live paycheck-to-paycheck is to have loads of debt and no money in the bank. Their monthly debt payments alone consume the majority of their income.

I see this all the time. As a financial coach, I meet with lots of married couples. Many of them are in their 30s and 40s looking for a way to undo many of the poor money decisions they've made in their early adult lives.

I'll give you an example that, unfortunately, resonates with too many people.

Recently, I had a couple in my office. Their minimum monthly payment on student loans was over $1000 a month. Every month. For the next 10 years. They had one child and one on the way. This mother wanted to transition into being a full-time stay-at-home-mom. Was I able to offer this young family a quick debt fix to reach their American Dream?

Sadly, no.

Instead, I had to look into the eyes of this young mother and basically tell her that, not only could she *not* stay home full-time, but she should probably increase her hours at work.

You see they came to me wanting a way to be free—free to live the life they wanted. But that decision was made years *ago* when they loaded themselves with student loan debt. The opportunity cost associated with debt usually extends far beyond just the minimum monthly payment.

On the flip-side, starting out in the "real world" without debt can open a plethora of opportunities that you may not fully realize until years down the road. Take my wife and me, for instance. As newlyweds, we had no idea that this crazy plan to be *Debtless* would be absolutely pivotal in allowing us to walk away from a career into unemployment eight years later without so much as breaking a sweat. We pursued the life we were called into. I found a new career path that fulfilled our purpose and we are continuing to live in freedom, encouraging others to do the same.

Being *Debtless* is hard, and not for the faint of heart. As they say, "If it was easy, everyone would do it." It's an intentional way of living that requires discipline. Trust me, I know. If you plan on finishing college and being *Debtless*, get ready for a season of saying "no" to excess and "yes" to sacrifice. You WILL go through a period of hardship.

*Debtless* will give you lots of real world tips for you live out that sacrifice. It won't be easy, but it will be worth it.

## PREFACE
By Josh Tayerle

I remember being 21 years old and thinking it was normal to graduate from college with $35,000 in student loan debt. I assumed I was going to easily make that much money my first year out of college while being able to put money into my savings account. Boy was I wrong. Even with a successful job right out of college, it was difficult to make ends meet.

After college, I started to experience those life issues I had heard older people complaining about. I started working two jobs to help pay for my food, rent, cell phone, cable TV, clothes, car insurance, health insurance, dental insurance, gas, and student loans with interest. I was living those dreaded words: paycheck to paycheck. I wasn't realistic with my budget and didn't include the cost of doing fun things like dating, going out with friends, or any other activities that cost money.

After a few years of working hard, I was able to put some money into my savings account. I thought I deserved a newer car, so I went to the bank and took out a small loan. I then added a car payment to my list of bills.

Later on, I met the love of my life and had to add the cost of dating, an engagement ring, a wedding, and a honeymoon to the budget. We gradually started spending more money than we were earning, which quickly drained our savings account. My wife and I decided to go back to the bank and take out another loan to help pay our monthly bills and our wedding.
The loan helped us pay our bills in the short term, but we had to pay back the loan with interest. Starting off our marriage in debt is by far the dumbest thing I have ever done. The loan that was supposed to help us pay our bills actually took more from us than just the interest. It took our time together.
I have learned that time is the most important thing that I value as I've gotten older. You can always make more money but you cannot get your time back. My wife understood that we had a bunch of debt with both of our student loans, both of our car payments, and our wedding loan, so she took a second job working overnights and weekends to help us pay our bills. We sacrificed our time together for our debt. We missed weddings, birthdays, and other fun events because we had to work.

If you're reading this book, please understand that buying a car, going on vacation, attending college, planning a wedding, purchasing a house, and other money decisions will impact the number of hours you have to work over the next 5, 10, 30+ years of your life.

The purpose of this book is to give you an inside look at how to become *Debtless*. When you have no debt, you're free to spend your time on the important things like family, friends, helping others, and pursuing your passions in life. By working hard and making sacrifices, Josiah has done just that. May his experiences guide you on your own journey to becoming *Debtless*.

## A NOTE FOR PARENTS

One evening about 18 years ago, you were holding a newborn child in your arms for the very first time. As you watched your peaceful little one sleep, your heart's desire was to see them grow up and have dreams of their own. No doubt these past years have gone by faster and faster.

Today, as you pick up this book with those same hands, your heart's desire hasn't changed. Funding college can be just as challenging and overwhelming for parents as it is for students, but planning and preparation can make it easier for everyone.

Parents are an important part of the *Debtless* process. Help your student discover and evaluate their options. Use this book as a tool to help you do that. This book is written for students, but that doesn't mean you can't benefit from it. Read along with your student and use it as a conversation starter.

To this day, my parents are my biggest cheerleaders and supporters. It meant the world to me that each time I transferred colleges, switched majors, worked jobs, and wrote out checks to pay for tuition, my parents respected me and told me they believed in me and were proud of me. My parents were a vital part of my education.

I believe everyone needs a coach. A good coach knows when to encourage their player and even calls them up to a higher level. Many times, if you treat your child like the person you know they have the potential to become, they will rise to the occasion. Along this journey together, encourage your child with the words: "I'm with you," "You can do this," "I believe in you," and "I'm proud of you."

One of my close friends told me that her parents had never gone to college. She felt alone in the process. With so little input from them, she had to figure things out herself. She ended up with a private, variable-rate loan that will take her years to pay off.

However overwhelmed or unequipped you feel as a parent, your child feels the same way. Likely, even more so. You don't have to stay where you are. You and your student can research, you can read, you can find the tools to succeed. Graduating college without student loans can be done.

So many students are taking out way too much in loans. This debt literally kills their dreams. I'm definitely an advocate for higher education. College is a great investment, and out of all of the types of debt you can take on, student debt can be an investment. The key is having a manageable debt load.

I speak with dozens of parents each year who are going through this journey. Many of them are single parents, others have kids who will be the first generation in their family tree to be college educated. It's perfectly normal to feel stressed out, anxious, and overwhelmed! The good news is, you don't have to do this alone. That's why I wrote this book. *Debtless* will help you and your student stay ahead on this journey.

Becoming *Debtless* is a lot like climbing Mount Everest—it's a lot of steps. Keep going. Take one step at a time.

## INTRODUCTION

I got my first job in high school, and my general manager gave me some advice that changed the trajectory of my life completely: "Josiah," he said, "Don't take out student loans. Work hard here, and work your way through college."

Fast forward to a few weeks after I graduated college completely debt free. The church where I had been volunteering for the last four years approached me with an offer. They wanted to hire me as the young adult pastor. There was just one catch—they couldn't pay me to start with. It was yet another volunteer position.

But I couldn't have cared less! It was my dream job. I was able to take it because I had no debt holding me back. I always think about that when I think about student loans—if I had had them, I most likely wouldn't have been able to take a job without a paycheck, even if it was what I had always wanted.

Ever since then, one of my passions has been seeing young people like you reach your dreams and full potential. It doesn't take long working with college students and twenty-somethings to see that you have big dreams. You want what you do to have purpose. But debt so often gets in the way of pursuing work that matters.

That's why I've spent two years of my life collecting stories and research on the topic of student loan debt. I want to see you start with less debt (or none at all) so you have nothing holding you back from realizing your dreams.

In this book, I'm going to share the research, stories, and tips I've gathered over the years. In Part 1, we'll talk about the debt problem and my survey of 850 current college students. In Part 2, I'll share 10 tips to help you start and stay debt-free in college.

Let's do this!

# PART 1: THE DEBT PROBLEM

The Minneapolis *Star Tribune* recently ran a story about a college student named Nikki. She's pursuing an associate's degree in Minnesota after attending a university in Missouri. So far, she's $140,000 in debt with no degree to show for it.

How did she get there? At the recommendation of a few teachers, she pursued her interest in journalism at an out-of-state school. She took out extra loans for rent, bills, and books, which her dad co-signed for. Now she works about 30 hours per week while taking classes at an in-state school. She wants to get married, but she doesn't want her boyfriend to take on her debt.

Nikki isn't alone in her situation. Dr. Shon is a 43-year-old surgeon with a son who's a freshman in college. Dr. Shon himself just paid off his student loans this year—just one month before his son started college! He said the amount he owed in student loans from medical school was just too much.

Student loan debt is a widespread problem that's holding many people back from pursuing their dreams and living their lives on their own terms. That's is why I chose to research this topic for my graduate school capstone project.

## RESEARCH FINDINGS

In 2016, I created a 17-question Debtless survey about student loan debt and distributed the link to hundreds of friends and strangers via social media. Responses from 850 current college students from 200 different colleges and universities in over 40 states paint a bleak picture of college financing.

Forty-five percent of students surveyed said they were not informed at all about alternatives to student loans. It was just assumed debt was their only option to finance their education. Only eighteen percent of students believed they were completely informed about the student loans they took out.

When it comes to loans, students have a few options—government loans and private loans.

Not all students qualify for government loans, and if you do qualify, the government limits how much you can borrow. A subsidized loan is a government loan that doesn't start accruing interest until you graduate college. An unsubsidized loan is a government loan that starts accruing interest as soon as you take it out. If you have to take out school loans, these are your best option.

You really need to be careful with private loans. If you can, avoid private student loans at all costs. There's no limit on what you can borrow, and you can end up with a variable-rate loan, which can really cost a lot more than you were planning to pay. Your interest will start accruing immediately. These are a higher-risk loan for banks because there's no guarantee of the student ever earning enough money to pay them back, so students are required to have a co-signer.

Thirty-nine percent of students surveyed have no idea how much they're taking out in student loans. Based on the *Debtless* survey, current students have taken on an average of $26,659 in student loans, and they haven't even graduated yet!

Other national research from studentloans.gov shows that for each year of college you're enrolled, the average loan taken out is $6,707. The average debt of a four-year college graduate is $26,830. The current average interest rate is at 6.8%.

When asked how much debt they have, *Debtless* survey responses ranged from as little as $0 to as much as $280,000, with dozens of responses totaling in the $100,000+ range.

Let's say you graduate college with the average amount in debt— $26,659. Based on the current average interest rate of 4.29%, you would owe $273.60 per month for 10 years. And over the course of those ten years, you'd pay a total of $32,832.

Or maybe you have one of the monster student loan amounts—you have $100,000 in debt. Your monthly payment would be would $1,026.29 for 10 years. Over the course of the loan, you would pay $123,154.80.

What if you end up with the grand total of $280,000 in student loans (and you have the income you need for food, shelter, and basic necessities)? This is a monthly payment of $2,873.61 for 10 years. In the end, you'd pay a total of $344,833.20.

Can you imagine what you would do if you had an extra $273.60, $1,026.29, or $2,873.61 per month in your budget to save, spend, and give over the course of 10 years because you didn't have student loan debt? This is exactly why it's important to take on the least amount of debt possible.

I asked respondents how they feel about the manageability of repaying their student loans. Only 34% said they believe repayment is completely manageable. Seven percent said repayment wouldn't be manageable.

Possibly the most important statistic I found is that nearly 40% of students were not informed at all on the alternatives to student debt. Only 11% were completely informed.

Financial advisor Michael Block says the number one issue he sees with young investors is student loans. If he were to give one piece of advice to young people, it would be to keep your debt as low as possible.

It's my hope that reading *Debtless* will help you stay on the right side of these statistics. In case you haven't figured it out yet, less debt is better than more debt! And being educated about your student loans and other financing options can make or break your future.

As a pastor to young adults, I see so many young people with passion and desire to chase their dreams, and the most common thing that holds them back is student loan debt. I had to put in a lot of hard work, but I was able to avoid that. I'm calling to you from the Promised Land—it's completely possible for you to live your dreams and achieve your financial goals as well. Make the necessary adjustments to your budget, your lifestyle, and your financial plan now so later you can experience freedom and ultimately chase your dreams!

## DISCUSS

1. Do you know anyone who's overwhelmed by debt or student loans?
2. What are you willing to do to avoid student loans?
3. What would you like to get out of reading this book? What are your own goals for financing your education?

# PART 2: PRACTICAL TIPS FOR MINIMIZING DEBT

## TIP #1: START THINKING ABOUT COLLEGE NOW

*"Do something today that your future self will thank you for."*
*—Sean Patrick Flanery*

When I was a high school freshman, my dad came to pick me up from a weight-training group I was part of. As he drove, he explained that something was different. We were riding in the same car as usual, he didn't have a new haircut, and his beard wasn't shaved, so I told him I gave up. That's when he told me he had been laid off from his job. My dad is the hardest worker I know. He didn't run his mouth at work and get fired, and he wasn't sent home for laziness. He had been a jeweler at the same company for over 20 years, but due to a downturn in the economy, the company had to make cutbacks financially.

My dad was our only source of income, and he was out of work for about six months. During this time, I learned God can provide in miraculous ways. We didn't lose our home, and we didn't miss a meal. There were times where the money was really tight and we didn't necessarily know where money for groceries would come from. But on more than one occasion, someone from our church taped money to our front door or anonymously mailed grocery store gift cards to our house. God always provided.

I can honestly say that I didn't know if going to college was a realistic expectation. Maybe you can relate. What I did know is that I liked baseball and I spent any spare cash I had to work on my "Joe Mauer swing" at the local batting cage, a place called Grand Slam. I ended up becoming such a frequent flyer there that the general manager offered me a job application when I was 14 years old and hadn't quite started high school yet.

I decided that day, in my dad's truck, at the age of 14, that I would get a job, buy my own car when I turned 16, and save for college. My older sister was about to graduate high school, and I knew from conversations I'd overheard that my parents weren't able to help her purchase a car or pay for college. But my dad's work ethic and diligence had a huge impact on me. When other kids were spending their money on things that helped them enjoy the moment, I decided to build up a savings account for college.

It's really never too soon to start thinking about college. The sooner you begin plan, the more time you have to work that plan. This will be to your benefit on your debtless jouney.

## DISCUSS

1. Do you want to go to college? Why or why not? What do you want to study?
2. Does your family have a plan to pay for college?
3. What can you do now to help you graduate with less debt later?

## TIP #2: FIND A MENTOR

*Everybody needs a Yoda!*

In *The Empire Strikes Back*, Luke Skywalker had a lot going on and needed some help. A small but wise mentor he found. As a high-ranking general and the Grand Master of the Jedi order, Yoda trained Luke to fight against the Galactic Empire. Do what Luke did—find a mentor. This is some of the best advice I can give you. Don't settle for just any person who's older than you. Find someone who has been where you want to go and can offer wisdom and advice to help you get there.

I love the ancient saying that says: "Walk with the wise and grow wise." There's value in seeking wisdom and counsel from older, more experienced people who have been where you want to go. I learned from a young age to ask as many questions as I could, to "go to school" through other people by learning from their successes and failures. I've heard it said, "Smart people learn from their own mistakes, but really smart people learn from other people's mistakes." That's what mentoring is all about.

In my own life, I was fortunate to meet a guy named Josh, who happened to be the general manager at Grand Slam, where I got my first job. He was like the cool, older brother I always wanted. I remember asking him a lot of big life questions. He was so practical and helpful, putting his real life experiences out there for me to learn from. He also had a strong vision, dreams, and direction for his life. He wanted to start a business, purchase a home, and get married, but his debt made those goals difficult to achieve.

Once I asked what he would do differently if he could do college all over again. He said he'd take on less debt in order to graduate from college. He'd gone to a very expensive private college and wished he hadn't taken on so many student loans.

Josh asked me some great questions and gave me advice, too. What was I spending my money on? He encouraged me to diligently save a percentage of every paycheck while I was in high school with almost no living expenses. He also helped me think about the big picture by explaining it takes about 10 years for the average person to pay off their college loans.

Josh suggested I start listening to Dave Ramsey, a personal money-management expert, who has a radio show and has written several books. I read *The Total Money Makeover* and listened to his show almost every day all through high school and college. His and Josh's advice helped me realize I wanted to graduate college without any student loans.

I can't thank Josh enough for the the experience, learning opportunities, and everything else he invested in me. Go find your own mentor who's been where you want to go. Ask questions. Learn from their successes and their failures. Their wisdom is more valuable than you realize.

## DISCUSS

1. Who do you know who's where you want to be in life? Who do you admire? Maybe they work the job you dream of, or they parent the way you've always wanted to lead.
2. Do you have a mentor? If not, who could be your mentor?
3. Would you be willing to mentor someone else someday?

### TIP #3: WORK WHILE YOU'RE IN SCHOOL

*"Find a job you enjoy doing, and you will never have to work a day in your life."*
—Mark Twain

There are academic, financial, and experiential benefits to working your way through school. Let's say you work 20 hours per week for $10 an hour. This adds up to $200 per week and $10,400 per year! That doesn't include any raises you might get or extra hours you could work during summer and winter breaks. Four years of work in college is worth about $41,600. That can go a long way!

Throughout high school and college, I worked at the same job at Grand Slam more than 20 hours per week on average. It was a great gig. They paid me well, which really helped pay for college. After four years in guest services, they also put me in their management program, and I worked as a store manager for another four years. The promotion came with better pay, more flexibility in my scheduling, great résumé experience, and the ability to hire about 30 students from my church. Not only was I able to put away a significant amount of money for college, I gained valuable skills and experiences you can't learn in a classroom.

I recently had the opportunity to meet financial expert Rachel Cruze. She's passionate about the value of working your way through college. One study she mentioned shows that students who have part-time jobs in college have higher grade point averages because they're required to manage their time well and prioritize their responsibilities.

How much Netflix do you watch in a week? Maybe instead of binge watching, you could work. For sure, it is hard work to manage classes, homework, a part-time job, and a social life, but I know personal experience that it is totally possible and totally worth it! Some of my favorite memories are from my time working at Grand Slam.

## DISCUSS

1. What's your financial situation? How much of your college expenses will you personally be responsible for?
2. Based on your schedule and responsibilities, how many hours could you reasonably work in a week?
3. Brainstorm some jobs where you could not only make money, but have fun and gain skills and experience.

## TIP #4: SAVE YOUR MONEY

*It's in your best interest not to pay interest!*

I love what Pastor Andy Stanley says about money: "Give 10%, Save 10%, Live on the rest." That means for every hundred dollars you earn, you should give $10, save $10, and use the remaining 80% to pay for groceries, housing, transportation, and travel. This is a great starting point for anyone looking to get a handle on their finances.

The thing about being a young person in high school—and maybe even college—is that your living expenses are probably a lot less than 80% of your income. You may only be working part time, but you can save a much higher percentage of your income for college expenses.

When I was in high school, most of my classmates had some sort of job. And most of them used their money to buy stuff—like expensive clothes, fast food, and the latest technology—and didn't even think about saving. Looking back, I am so thankful that I listened to the friendly advice of my mentor—Josh had my best interest in mind when he told me to save as much as I could. I saved about 80% of my income for two things—a $3500 Jeep that I paid cash for and my college education.

I also worked enough in college to pay for my bills. At one point I felt like I was running out of savings because I was writing checks to pay for college. I asked my dad if I should take out loans or take a break from school to build my savings account back up. He told me something I'll never forget: "Having zero in the bank is better than debt."

So often I hear people say, "I wish someone had told me when I was younger," or, "I wish they would have taught us this in school." That's why I'm writing this book. The less debt you have, the better. And, if you can make it through college completely *Debtless*, you'll be able to pursue your dreams. It's like Dave Ramsey often says: "If you will live like no one else, later you can live like no one else." Do what seems crazy now and you'll reap the benefits in the long run.

## DISCUSS

1. Think about how you spend your money. Do you give and save before you spend?
2. What are your living expenses? How much could you reasonably save if you worked the number of hours you came up with at the end of Tip #3?
3. Think about life after college. If you could graduate debt free, what could you do that those with debt aren't able to do?

## TIP #5: GET A HEAD START

*"Discipline, not desire, determines your destiny."*
—Andy Stanley

A doctor friend has a saying that I've honorably adopted: "An ounce of preventative measure is worth a gallon of cure." This is obviously true in the medical field. If people drink water, eat healthy, and exercise regularly, they're a lot less likely to have medical emergencies later on in life. Being disciplined on the front end is a lot more effective than surgery, radiation, or other medical interventions after you've already developed a medical condition.

This lesson translates to finances as well: start working now, start saving now, do what you can ahead of time to gain a head start.

I had a few head starts. The best one was taking college classes while I was still in school through Postsecondary Enrollment Options (PSEO). Basically I got to take college classes for free while I was still in high school. I had to twist my parent's arms to convince them, but we talked to my guidance counselor. During my junior and senior years of high school, I started my days out with classes at a local community college and ended my days with classes at my high school. When I graduated high school, I had an associate's degree under my belt. And I didn't pay anything for it! Those credits transferred to the university I attended and I ended up with a bachelor's degree for about half the cost.

More and more students are getting some type of early start on college that helps them complete a four-year bachelor's degree in three years or less. I can see this becoming more common—who wouldn't want to take advantage of an opportunity that can save you so much money?

Most high schools offer some version of this program. If you were able to take one class worth three college credits while you're in high school, you would save about $1,500. I know several students—myself included—who had 60 credits toward college by the time they graduated high school! This was dollar-for-dollar the biggest reason I was able to graduate college *Debtless*.

Think about when you were a kid playing hide and seek with your friends on the playground. You would give people a head start hiding. The longer the head start, the better potential hiding places.

College is like that. The government and universities are allowing students like you to get a head start earning college credits, so take advantage of it! The longer the head start, the better the end result, and the less debt you'll have. So what are you waiting for?

## DISCUSS

1. What are some ways you can begin earning college credit now? Have you already started?
2. What could your life look like if you got a head start on college?
3. What's your plan for paying for college?

## TIP #6: VISIT THE GUIDANCE OFFICE

*You have everything to gain and nothing to lose by applying for scholarships. The worst thing they can say is no!*

One of the best things you can do to get a head start on college finances is visit your guidance counselor—someone who has a heart to see students succeed. He or she will have a ton of resources to help you find the right school and get a head start on financing your education. You can learn about college courses you can take while you're in high school, national and local scholarship opportunities, and other ways you can get a head start on college.

Applying for scholarships and earning college credits early may seem daunting now, but they'll pay dividends with your time and your money. If you get awarded a $500 scholarship that took you two hours to apply for, you just made $250 per hour! I'm confident that if you're reading this book, you can find at least one scholarship to apply for that's worth at least $500. Probably more! It's worth the effort. Later on, you'll get to spend less time in a classroom and less money on your tuition.

There are a ton of other ways you can earn college credit without the bill. AP classes, like PSEO, allow you to earn college credit while you're in high school based on the results of an AP test you take at the end of the year. Unlike PSEO, you take them at your high school.

CLEP tests are another great option. You can pay a couple hundred dollars to test out of a class. If you pass, you earn the credits for that class. I know students who "CLEP out" of as many as a half-dozen classes. They save about a semester's worth of time and thousands of dollars. In my experience, the closer to high school you take them, the better.

Other opportunities include College in the Schools, honors courses, and International Baccalaureate. Your guidance counselor will know all about these opportunities and more to help you start off on the right foot.

When you meet with your counselor, ask these questions:
1. How can I start earning college credits now?
2. How can I apply for scholarships today?
3. What other opportunities am I eligible for that would help me pay for college?

## DISCUSS

1. What can you do financially today that you'll thank yourself for later?
2. What are some ways you can start earning college credit now?
3. Who can you talk to at your school who can help you get a head start?

## TIP #7: FOLLOW A BUDGET

*Don't allow debt to hold you back from your dream.*

In the introduction, I told the story of how I had to work as a volunteer in my dream job for six months before I was able to earn a paycheck. There is literally no way I could have done that if I hadn't been in a place of financial freedom.

Dreams like that require sacrifice and discipline. For me, it took discipline while I was in high school and college, working and making wise financial choices so I wouldn't end up with student loans. It also meant I had to continue working part time while I volunteered in my dream job. None of that would have made a difference if I hadn't learned how to budget my money and plan how I was going to spend and save it.

I've talked to quite a few young adults who found creative ways to stretch their money while in college. Stephen is one of my favorite examples. When he came to the Twin Cities for college, he lived with his uncle, who didn't have Internet. Not a great situation for a college student. But Stephen worked part time and really enjoyed coffee from Starbucks. Instead of paying for internet at home *and* paying for coffee, he would study and hang out at coffee shops where he could enjoy his coffee and take advantage of complimentary wifi.

My sister Jerusha worked as a Resident Advisor, a position that paid for her room and board, drastically lowering the cost of attending college and living on campus. She saw me live at home and didn't want to miss out on the valuable experiences living on campus had to offer. The leadership experience she gained also looks great on her résumé!

Another student I know, Harrison, is a phenomenal musician who attended a prestigious music college on the east coast. It only took a year for him to realize how much money he was spending. When he calculated his expected income after graduation, he decided to move back home with his parents and take online classes at the same school instead. The cost of three years at home with his parents, working and taking online classes, equaled the cost of living on campus for one year. He made a really wise decision.

When I was in college, I didn't have a meal plan. My friend Micah didn't either. My first semester of college, we got into the habit of eating in Dinkytown, a neighborhood by the University of Minnesota, almost every day. From Schweng Cheng to Qdoba to Mesa Pizza to Five Guys, we had some really good food and great memories building a rock-solid friendship together over food.

But when it got to the end of the semester, I looked at my bank account and realized I'd been spending about $50 per week—just on lunch. It added up to $200 per month and well over $500 over the course of the semester. Spending all that money on food is one of the least thoughtful things I've done financially.

Don't make the same mistake I did. Create a budget and stick to it. Tell your money where to go rather than wondering where it went.

## DISCUSS

1. Do you know how to create a budget? Do you use one now?
2. What's the difference between needing something and wanting something? What things will you need in college? What things are just wants?
3. How can you make more money and/or reduce spending right now?


## TIP #8: LIVE AT HOME

*"There's no place like home."*
*—Dorothy Gale*

Another way you can save big on college expenses is living at home. Yes, commuting has it's own expenses—a car, repairs, insurance, and gas—but the savings are worth it. Over the course of the three years I was in college, I paid about half of what I would have paid if I lived on campus.

This is the most controversial tip in this book. Over the years, I've gotten a lot of feedback from parents, students, and experts about the value of the college campus experience. I don't deny that living on campus can be a valuable experience.

Here's how I respond to that: these aren't the only 10 tips, or even the best 10 tips, on how to minimize college debt and graduate debt free. This is me writing based on my own experience and research. It's how I did it, but it's not the only way to become *Debtless*.

As an extrovert and people person, I recognize the unique benefits of living on campus: you can definitely experience powerful community life with life-long relationships. But I also know what it is to make sacrifices to pursue my dreams. Along the way, there are sacrifices you need to make, and either way there's a price to pay. I chose to sacrifice the on-campus social life during my college years so I could live at home and save money. Plenty of other folks have chosen to spend extra, take out student loans, and live on campus. Some will tell you it was worth it. The fact remains that living on campus can save you a ton of money if that's the route you choose to go.

Maybe you could live at home for your first year or two, taking general credits at a community college and working. Similarly, finding an in-state school will generally allow you to pay in-state tuition, which is lower than out-of-state expenses. In some states, you can actually be from any bordering state to receive the lower tuition rate. Each state is a little different, so be sure to do your research, but if you can find a school with your preferred major program and pay in-state tuition, it will lower your cost.

Out-of-state tuition is a different story. Harrison—one of the students I mentioned in Tip #7—experienced this. He was a resident in Minnesota and went off to his dream school in Boston for his dream major—music.

He lived on campus for one year. The out-of-state tuition, higher cost of living, and already-expensive school led him to make a very difficult decision. He moved back to Minnesota, got a part-time job, and continued his education through the same school, online rather than on campus. This was thinking creatively. Three years online was the same cost as one year on campus. Many schools offer online programs that can save you a lot of money on tuition.

For whatever reason, you might prefer to live on campus to soak up every minute of the college experience. You know what? Go for it! This book isn't about money, it's about pursuing your dreams. But plan for it. Save for living on campus. Budget for living on campus. Pick up an extra job, become an R.A., save money over the summer. You can totally live on campus and still graduate without student loans, it just takes extra intentionality and planning!

## DISCUSS

1. Is living at home an option for you?
2. How else can you lower your living expenses while taking classes?
3. Could you take general classes at a community college and then transfer to a different college or university?

## TIP #9: BUY YOUR BOOKS ONLINE

*There are so many creative ways to earn and save money for college. Use the hashtag #DebtlessBook and share yours!*

Did you know buying your textbooks online rather than at the school bookstore can save you hundreds of dollars each semester?

When I first went to college, I was so excited to go to the bookstore. They made it so convenient to sign a paper and get my books right there—for several hundred dollars. But, it's the cost of college, right? After I spent the money, I learned I could have gotten the same books used from Amazon for a lot cheaper. Other great options include renting textbooks from your college or university. Some students have told us that they bought their textbooks used from upperclassmen. Use whatever option works best for you!

After that, on average, I saved around $300 per semester by ordering used books online instead of getting new ones at the bookstore. If you can save $300 each semester, that's at least $2,400 you're saving over the course of four years!

At the end of each semester, you can sell your books and recoup some of your expenses. It's up to you if you want to keep them, but you'll probably have some you won't need anymore. You might even get lucky and sell a few of them for more than you paid! Amazon has a program that gives you a gift card if you sell them your books at the end of the semester. Many bookstores do book buybacks, too, though you can usually get more for your books online. Don't expect to make a lot of money selling books, but it can help cover the cost of books for the next semester!

# DISCUSS

1. How much do textbooks cost for your major?
2. Do you know anyone who might be willing to loan or sell you their books?
3. What other creative ways have you heard about or thought of that could save you money?

## TIP #10: GIVE

*"Become fluent in the language of generosity and you'll always be rich."*
—Brent Silkey

Probably the last thing you'd expect to hear from a guy writing a book about avoiding debt would be a chapter on the importance of giving. But generosity is a key component of this book!

I'm not writing this book so you can stack up piles of money for yourself. I want to see you take on less debt, save more, pursue your dreams, and ultimately give generously to make a difference in other people's lives.

When I graduated college, a group of my friends and I set out to run 100 miles in four days to raise money to feed refugee kids in Burma. I set a goal to raise $1,000 and ended up collecting about $1,400. With the help of our church, we raised over $100,000!

It was the most difficult physical challenge of my life—essentially four back-to-back marathons. During the hardest part of the run, I felt like giving up. My body was failing—my lungs were screening for oxygen, and my legs felt like Jell-O that had been lit on fire. I thought of the people I might never meet who would receive nutritious meals because of what I was doing. I'll never forget what happened inside of me when I moved beyond my needs, wants, and preferences to make a difference for others.

In *A Christmas Carol*, Ebenezer Scrooge chased after money. That's what mattered to him. In the end, he got a second chance at life and a new understanding of gratitude that allowed him to experience the joy of Christmas. He began sharing his money with others in need.

Zacchaeus was a tax collector in ancient Israel. Back in those days, tax collectors took extra for themselves. The general public saw them as thieves, and Zacchaeus was no different. He amassed an incredible amount of financial wealth from robbing his fellow men. After a visit from Jesus, Zacchaeus was a changed man. He not only gave back what he had wrongfully stolen, but he gave back four times what he had taken.

Both Zacchaeus and Scrooge show us how money can influence our lives. We might not have the chance to see the past, present, and future flash before our eyes in dreams or visions, and Jesus may not pay us a visit to point out where we need to be changed from the inside out, but how we handle our money can transform our lives.

My hope is that you will experience gratitude and give with a generous heart now. When debt isn't holding you back, you can live and give in a more generous way. I recommend giving while trying to stay out of debt to develop and grow your generosity muscles.

Habits start now. I'd rather see you give away money you have than spend money you don't have. I would rather see you start good habits now. The habits you create in college have a tendency of following you and becoming lifelong habits. Debt and borrowing are a poor habit. Giving and cultivating a habit of generosity are great habits!

## DISCUSS

1. What are some causes you believe in?
2. What does generosity mean to you?
3. Do you think you're living greedy, grateful, or somewhere in the middle?

## DREAM

*"What would you try if you knew you could not fail?"*
—Ryan Leak

This is my final tip for you: think about your life goals and dreams. The whole concept of *Debtless* began as a dream for me. I wanted to graduate college without any student loans. Now, I never want to stop dreaming. If you're like me and you have dreams, they're not in your heart to tease you. They're there so you can make them happen. You can reach your dreams—it's possible! So chase them with reckless abandon and don't allow debt to hold you back. Following these tips will help you get there:

Talk to your parents or a mentor about your dreams. They can be your biggest cheerleaders, supporters, and encouragers. **If college is a dream of yours, start thinking and planning toward that today!** The time to start is now.

Talk to someone who's doing what you want to be doing someday. How did they get there? Do they have any recommendations that could help you get there yourself? If you want to be an author, find an author you respect on twitter and reach out to them. If your dream is to be an engineer, contact someone who works at 3M or another major engineering company and pick their brain. Most people are honored and flattered when you reach out and ask them for help or insight. **Find a mentor. Everybody needs a Yoda**!

My hope is that you would minimize and avoid student loans and other types of debt. But that's not an end in and of itself. I want you to have the chance to pursue your dreams and impact the world around you in significant ways. One of the best ways that I found to avoid loans was working a job in both high school and college. **Go ahead and work while you're in school!**
I always follow up talking about work with talking about savings. I'm thankful my grandpa Joe and my parents taught me the value of savings. Whenever you have a dream, there is a cost. If you can save for it in advance and pay cash, it'll accelerate the pace. **Save your money!**

Do you feel a sense of urgency yet? I'm proud of you and honored that you stuck with me this far along in the book. I wanted it to be brief and to the point. Getting a head start is will help you achieve your dreams in less time with less expense. **A person with a head start in a race has the advantage. Start now!**

I'm a big advocate of asking for directions, advice, insight, and counsel. I've always felt at home around people who know what they're doing. Visit your high school's guidance office and tell them I sent you. **Ask how you can earn college credit and apply for scholarships today!**

On your journey, you'll find you need to pause at different mile markers, just like on a road trip. Whenever you travel a distance, long or short, it's helpful to have a map or GPS. **Financially speaking, your budget is your roadmap. Make one and follow it!**

It's ultimately up to you, but one of the biggest ways I saved on the cost of my college tuition was living at home. **Try to find a way to live at home, pay in-state tuition, or go to a community college!**

No matter who you are **buying your textbooks online is an instant money saver!**

I'd rather see you give away money that you have than spend money that you don't have. Cultivate good habits now. Debt and borrowing are bad habits. **Give and live generously instead!**

From here on, it's really up to you. Pursue your dreams and write the rest of your own story!

## DISCUSS

1. What is your dream?
2. Where do you want to be a year from now? Four years from now?
3. Who can help you get there?

# HOW I BECAME DEBTLESS

set a goal and pursued it intentionally.

While in high school, I took an AP class and many classes through PSEO. I spent only three years at a university rather than four. That cut my costs by 25%.

worked in high school and saved as much as I could to pay for college.

worked 20–30 hours (more during breaks) when I was in college.

lived at home. This cut my costs by about half. This was quite possibly my greatest sacrifice, but it was worth it.

## ABOUT THE AUTHOR

Josiah Kennealy is the young adults pastor at Cedar Valley Church in Bloomington, Minnesota. He's passionate about helping young people find Jesus, grow in their faith, become *Debtless*, and pursue their God-given dreams. When he's not at church, you can find him watching the Twins, studying leadership, or working out.

Josiah has appeared on The Dave Ramsey Show and frequently speaks to students and young adults about finances and the importance of staying out of debt.

## FIND JOSIAH AND DEBTLESS ONLINE

Facebook | JosiahKennealy, DebtlessBook
Twitter | @JosiahKennealy
Instagram | @JosiahKennealy
YouTube | @JosiahKennealy
josiahkennealy.com

# ACKNOWLEDGEMENTS

Jesus, my savior and audience of one. My personal relationship with you has forever changed my life. My sin was a great debt. You have paid my debt, and I am eternally *Debtless*!

To the anonymous 850 current college students who took the research survey for my graduate studies capstone project, thank you! You helped me write this book for other students just like you.

I asked a group of 20 or so friends to be my prayer partners for this project. Asking for your help was my first step in writing *Debtless*. Thank you for your prayer support.

One of my guilty pleasures is hanging out on social media, and about 500 people joined my social media/promo team for *Debtless*. I am blessed by your generosity in sharing this with others!

Sarah Young, thanks a ton for believing in this process from the get-go and for editing this project. Each reader can thank you for making this content readable! (If you're a writer, I can't recommend her more highly.)

Brandon Eckroth, thank you for letting me use your crazy talents with the camera to capture the cover photo.

David Nguyen, I appreciate your work on the graphic design and layout. People judge a book by the cover, and I really like this one.

My friend, Lincoln Poole, thanks for your help shooting, creating, and editing the book trailer and content for the web!

Made in the USA
Monee, IL
08 February 2021